STECK-VAUGHN

Level D

LANGUAGE Exercises

TEACHER'S GUIDE

Betty Jones

Saranna Moeller

Cynthia T. Strauch

STECK-VAUGHN
ELEMENTARY • SECONDARY • ADULT • LIBRARY
A Harcourt Company

www.steck-vaughn.com

Table of Contents

Acknowledgments

Executive Editor: Diane Sharpe
Supervising Editor: Stephanie Muller
Project Editor: Patricia Claney
Design Manager: Laura Cole

LANGUAGE EXERCISES Series:

Level A	Level D	Level G
Level B	Level E	Level H
Level C	Level F	Review

ISBN 0-8114-6317-6

6 7 8 9 RP 02 01

Introduction

Language Exercises is a program designed for students who require additional practice in the basics of effective writing and speaking. Focused practice in key grammar, usage, mechanics, and composition areas helps students gain ownership of essential skills. The logical sequence of the practice exercises, combined with a clear and concise format, allows for easy and independent use.

Focus on Key Skills

Language Exercises provides systematic, focused attention to just one carefully selected skill at a time. Rules are clearly stated at the beginning of each lesson. Key terms are introduced in bold type. The rules are then illustrated with examples and followed by meaningful practice exercises.

Lessons are organized around a series of units. They are arranged in a logical sequence beginning with vocabulary, progressing through sentences, grammar and usage, mechanics, and culminating with composition skills.

Levels C through H and Review include a final unit on study skills, which can be assigned as needed. This unit includes such skills as organizing information, following directions, using a dictionary, using the library, and choosing appropriate reference sources.

Skills are reviewed thoroughly in a two-page Review at the conclusion of each unit and in the twelve-page Final Review at the end of the book. Also, the last twelve pages of this Teacher's Guide provide six two-page blackline master Unit Tests presented in a standardized test format. The content of each unit is repeated and expanded in subsequent levels as highlighted in the Scope and Sequence chart on the next two pages.

Application Is the Key

Throughout the program, *Language Exercises* stresses the application of language principles. In addition to matching, circling, or underlining elements in a predetermined sentence, lessons ask students to use what they have learned in an original sentence or in rewriting a sentence. *Using What You've Learned,* a two-page lesson at the end of each unit, provides students with an opportunity to "pull together" what they have learned in the unit and apply their learning to a writing situation.

Easy-to-Use Lessons

From the beginning, students feel comfortable with the format of the lessons. Each lesson is introduced with a rule at the top of the page and ends with a meaningful exercise at the bottom of the page. Each lesson is clearly labeled, and directions are clear and uncomplicated. Because the format is logical and consistent and the vocabulary is carefully controlled, most students can use *Language Exercises* with a high degree of independence. As the teacher, this allows you the time needed to help students on a one-to-one basis.

Attention to Composition Skills

The process approach to teaching writing provides success for most students. *Language Exercises* provides direct support for the teaching of composition and significantly enhances those strategies and techniques commonly associated with the process-writing approach.

Each book includes a composition unit that provides substantial work with important composition skills, such as writing topic sentences, selecting supporting details, taking notes, writing reports, and revising and proofreading. Also included in the composition unit is practice with various prewriting activities, such as clustering and brainstorming, which play an important role in process writing. The composition lessons are presented in the same rule-plus-practice format as in other units.

Teacher's Guide

The Teacher's Guide for each level of *Language Exercises* includes a two-page Scope and Sequence chart and an Answer Key in an easy-to-use format for all exercises.

The final section of the Teacher's Guide includes six two-page blackline master Unit Tests presented in a standardized test format. The skills and concepts included on these tests parallel the skills in the end-of-unit Reviews in the student book. These Unit Tests can also be used as both pre- and post-tests. Answers for these tests appear on the final page of the Answer Key.

SCOPE AND SEQUENCE

	A	B	C	D	E	F	G	H	Review
Vocabulary									
Sound Words (Onomatopoeia)	■								
Rhyming Words	■	■							
Synonyms	■	■	■	■	■	■	■	■	■
Antonyms	■	■	■	■	■	■	■	■	■
Homonyms	■	■	■	■	■	■	■	■	■
Multiple Meanings/Homographs	■	■	■	■	■	■	■	■	■
Prefixes and Suffixes			■	■	■	■	■	■	■
Base and Root Words			■	■	■	■	■	■	■
Compound Words			■	■	■	■	■	■	■
Contractions			■	■	■	■	■	■	■
Idioms						■	■	■	■
Connotation/Denotation						■	■	■	■
Sentences									
Word Order in Sentences	■	■							
Recognizing a Sentence	■	■	■	■	■	■	■	■	■
Subjects and Predicates	■	■	■	■	■	■	■	■	■
Types of Sentences	■	■	■	■	■	■	■	■	■
Compound/Complex Sentences			■	■	■	■	■	■	■
Sentence Combining			■	■	■	■	■	■	■
Run-On Sentences				■	■	■	■	■	■
Independent and Subordinate Clauses							■	■	■
Compound Subjects and Predicates						■	■	■	■
Direct and Indirect Objects							■	■	■
Inverted Word Order						■	■	■	■
Grammar and Usage									
Common and Proper Nouns	■	■	■	■	■	■	■	■	■
Singular and Plural Nouns	■	■	■	■	■	■	■	■	■
Possessive Nouns				■	■	■	■	■	■
Appositives						■	■	■	■
Verbs	■	■	■	■	■	■	■	■	■
Verb Tense	■	■	■	■	■	■	■	■	■
Regular/Irregular Verbs	■	■	■	■	■	■	■	■	■
Subject/Verb Agreement		■	■	■	■	■	■	■	■
Verb Phrases						■	■	■	■
Transitive and Intransitive Verbs							■	■	■
Verbals: Gerunds, Participles, and Infinitives							■	■	■
Active and Passive Voice							■	■	■
Mood								■	■
Pronouns	■	■	■	■	■	■	■	■	■
Antecedents							■	■	■
Articles	■	■	■						
Adjectives	■	■	■	■	■	■	■	■	■
Correct Word Usage (e.g. *may/can, sit/set*)	■	■	■	■	■	■	■	■	■
Adverbs			■	■	■	■	■	■	■
Prepositions					■	■	■	■	■
Prepositional Phrases						■	■	■	■
Conjunctions						■	■	■	■
Interjections						■	■	■	
Double Negatives								■	■
Capitalization and Punctuation									
Capitalization: First Word in Sentence	■	■	■	■	■	■	■		■
Capitalization: Proper Nouns	■	■	■	■	■	■	■	■	■
Capitalization: in Letters		■	■	■	■	■	■	■	■
Capitalization: Abbreviations		■	■	■	■	■	■	■	■
Capitalization: Titles		■	■	■	■	■	■	■	■

	A	B	C	D	E	F	G	H	Review
Capitalization and Punctuation (cont'd)									
Capitalization: Proper Adjectives					■	■	■	■	■
End Punctuation	■	■	■	■	■	■	■	■	■
Commas		■	■	■	■	■	■	■	■
Apostrophes in Contractions		■	■	■	■	■	■	■	■
Apostrophes in Possessives			■	■	■	■	■	■	■
Quotation Marks			■	■	■	■	■	■	■
Colons/Semicolons						■	■	■	■
Hyphens						■	■	■	■
Composition									
Expanding Sentences					■	■	■	■	■
Writing a Paragraph		■	■	■	■	■	■	■	■
Paragraphs: Topic Sentence (main idea)		■	■	■	■	■	■	■	■
Paragraphs: Supporting Details		■	■	■	■	■	■	■	■
Order In Paragraphs		■	■	■	■	■	■		■
Writing Process:									
Establishing Purpose			■	■		■	■	■	■
Audience					■	■	■	■	■
Topic			■	■	■	■	■	■	■
Outlining				■		■	■	■	■
Clustering/Brainstorming					■		■	■	■
Notetaking						■	■		
Revising/Proofreading					■	■	■	■	■
Types of Writing:									
Poem	■								
Letter	■	■	■			■			
"How-to" Paragraph			■						
Invitation			■						
Telephone Message			■						
Conversation				■					
Narrative Paragraph				■					
Comparing and Contrasting					■				
Descriptive Paragraph					■				
Report						■			
Interview							■		
Persuasive Composition								■	■
Readiness/Study Skills									
Grouping	■								
Letters of Alphabet	■								
Listening	■	■							
Making Comparisons	■	■							
Organizing Information	■	■	■						
Following Directions	■	■	■	■	■				
Alphabetical Order	■	■	■	■	■	■	■	■	■
Using a Dictionary:									
Definitions		■	■	■	■	■	■	■	■
Guide Words/Entry Words		■	■	■	■	■	■	■	■
Syllables			■	■	■	■	■	■	■
Pronunciation			■	■	■	■	■	■	■
Multiple Meanings				■	■	■	■	■	■
Word Origins						■	■	■	■
Parts of a Book			■	■	■	■	■	■	■
Using the Library						■	■	■	■
Using Encyclopedias				■	■	■	■	■	■
Using Reference Books						■	■	■	■
Using the *Readers' Guide*							■	■	■
Using Tables, Charts, Graphs, and Diagrams						■	■	■	■
Choosing Appropriate Sources						■	■	■	■

Answer Key

Unit 1 Vocabulary

Lesson 1, Synonyms (P. 1)

A. **1.** desire
2. outdoors
3. seeing
4. write
5. match
6. ask
7. ideas
8. little
9. enjoy
10. grew
11. arranged

B. **1.** The common hive has many worker bees.
2. It is not uncommon to find 80,000 active workers in a colony.
3. The brave worker bee will do anything to halt the enemies of the hive.
4. The hive must stay warm, or the bees will die.
5. Farmers are glad to see large hives near their fields.

Lesson 2, Antonyms (P. 2)

A. **1.** sharp **2.** soft **3.** wrong **4.** save **5.** forget **6.** messy **7.** begin **8.** new **9.** top

B. Answers will vary. Suggested antonyms: big, clean, good, cleaned, brighten, drying, wrong, same

Lesson 3, Homonyms (P. 3)

A. **1.** its **2.** it's **3.** it's **4.** it's **5.** its **6.** its **7.** it's **8.** its **9.** it's

B. **1.** There **2.** They're **3.** they're **4.** their **5.** there **6.** Their **7.** they're **8.** their

Lesson 4, More Homonyms (P. 4)

A. **1.** two, to **2.** too, to **3.** to **4.** two

B. **1.** write **2.** right **3.** right **4.** right

C. **1.** hear **2.** here, hear **3.** here, hear **4.** here

Lesson 5, Multiple Meanings (P. 5)

A. **1.** pillow
2. salty liquid from the eye
3. strike over and over
4. make the sound of a bell
5. loud noise
6. heavy winds with rain or snow
7. guide

B. Sentences will vary.

Lesson 6, Prefixes (P. 6)

A. **1.** disappear **2.** unconcerned **3.** unaware **4.** discover **5.** unharmed **6.** dislike **7.** disagree

B. **1.** misunderstood **2.** misuse **3.** recreate **4.** relive **5.** misjudged **6.** react

Lesson 7, Suffixes (P. 7)

A. **1.** successful **2.** tireless **3.** effortless **4.** careless **5.** meaningful **6.** endless **7.** worthless **8.** joyless

B. **1.** without color **2.** without a bottom **3.** full of sorrow **4.** full of beauty **5.** without flavor

Lesson 8, Compound Words (P. 8)

A. **1.** week, end **2.** home, made **3.** water, melon **4.** sun, set

B. **1.** tugboat **2.** waterfront **3.** loudspeaker **4.** watchman **5.** fireplace

C. Sentences will vary. Suggested compound words: newspaper, midnight, notebook, baseball

Lesson 9, Contractions (P. 9)

A. **1.** I'll **2.** we've **3.** You'll **4.** she's **5.** he's

B. **1.** can not **2.** did not **3.** will not **4.** is not **5.** we will

Review (P. 10)

A. Sentences will vary. Suggested synonyms:
1. big; little **2.** scared; odd

B. **1.** whole; entire
2. built; constructed

C. Answers will vary. Suggested antonyms:
1. large; hot **2.** new; laugh

D. **1.** wise **2.** sad **3.** sadden

E. 1. hear
2. two; to
3. It's; its
4. write; right
5. their; there

F. 1. moving air   2. to coil or turn

Review (P. 11)

G. Sentences will vary.

H. 1. disagree; returning
2. thoughtless; misuse
3. thankful; unlimited

I. 1. air-conditioned
2. haircut
3. doorknob

J. 1. I would; I am
2. he is; does not
3. did not; she would

Using What You've Learned (P. 12)

A. Paragraphs will vary.

B. Line 2. here; too
Line 3. to
Line 4. There
Line 5. It's
Line 6. two
Line 7. hear
Line 8. they're
Line 9. right

C. Sentences will vary.

Using What You've Learned (P. 13)

D. 1. I am unhappy with the way the tape sounds.
2. I was hopeful that this tape would be good.
3. Now it seems that I misjudged it.
4. I'm still unsatisfied/dissatisfied with the way it sounds.

E. Sentences will vary. Suggested compound words: campfire, firelight, flashlight, postcard, flashcard, lightpost

F. 1. isn't   is not
2. wouldn't   would not
3. She's   She is
4. can't   can not
5. we're   we are

Unit 2 Sentences

Lesson 10, Recognizing a Sentence (P. 14)

A. 1. S
2. S
4. S
5. S
8. S

B. 1. S
2. Sentences will vary.
3. S
4. Sentences will vary.
5. S

Lesson 11, Declarative and Interrogative (P. 15)

A. 1. interrogative
2. declarative
3. declarative
4. interrogative
5. declarative
6. interrogative
7. declarative
8. interrogative
9. declarative
10. interrogative
11. interrogative
12. declarative
13. interrogative
14. declarative
15. interrogative
16. interrogative
17. declarative
18. declarative

B. Sentences will vary.

Lesson 12, Changing Sentences (P. 16)

A. 1. Am I finished?
2. Shouldn't you be finished?
3. Is this taking too long?
4. Are you leaving?
5. Can you stay?

B. Sentences may vary. Suggested:
1. Does Joe start his new job today?
2. Does he begin at nine o'clock?
3. Will he leave home at eight o'clock?
4. Does Joe like to work on cars?
5. Is repairing cars very interesting?
6. Is Joe sure he will like this job?
7. Will Joe do a good job?

Lesson 13, Imperative and Exclamatory (P. 17)

A. 1. imperative
2. imperative
3. exclamatory
4. imperative
5. exclamatory
6. exclamatory
7. imperative
8. imperative
9. exclamatory
10. exclamatory
11. imperative
12. imperative

B. Sentences will vary.

Lesson 14, Subjects and Predicates (P. 18)

A. Subjects will vary.

B. Predicates will vary.

C. 1. subject
2. predicate
3. predicate
4. subject
5. predicate
6. subject
7. predicate

D. 1. Tennis was invented by Major Walter Wingfield.
2. The game was called tennis-on-the-lawn.
3. Mary Outerbridge brought the game to the United States.
4. Tennis is a popular game.
5. Steffi Graf is a famous tennis player.
6. You can play tennis, too.

Lesson 15, Simple Subjects and Predicates (P. 19)

A. Students should circle the words in bold.
1. The **plans** for a new car are made years ahead of time.
2. Many important **decisions** go into the design of a car.
3. Each **part** of the car is studied.
4. A clay **model** is made to show what the car will look like.

B. Students should circle words in bold.
1. Seven kinds of bears **live** in the world.
2. Most bears **live** in areas north of the equator.
3. Bears **have** small eyes.
4. Bears **can live** as long as thirty years.
5. A bear **uses** its claws to dig for food.
6. Brown bears usually **eat** grasses, berries, and nuts.
7. Seals and other animals **are** food for a polar bear.
8. Most bears **sleep** all winter.
9. Pandas **are** not really bears at all.

C.

	Subject	Predicate
1.	game	was played
2.	teams	played
3.	game	was

Lesson 16, Simple and Compound Sentences (P. 20)

A.
1. compound
2. compound
3. simple
4. simple
5. compound
6. simple
7. simple
8. compound
9. compound
10. simple

B. Sentences will vary.

Lesson 17, Combining Sentences (P. 21)

A. Sentences may vary. Suggested:
1. We have to write a history report.
2. My subject is the Civil War and Robert E. Lee.
3. We must use the encyclopedia and other books.
4. I should stop wasting time and start my report.

B. Sentences may vary. Suggested:
1. Juan bought a big brown horse.
2. The horse is kept in an old red barn.
3. Juan and Lynn ride the horse in a field.

C. Sentences will vary.

Lesson 18, Avoiding Run-on Sentences (P. 22)

Answers may vary. Some possible sentences follow.
1. One morning we found a baby bird.
2. It had been knocked from its nest by high winds.
3. Its mother was nowhere to be seen.
4. It was too young to fly.
5. We took it inside to care for it.
6. We were excited about taking care of the bird.
7. We didn't know what to do about feeding it.

Answers may vary. Suggested:
1. The bird's little mouth flew open so often that we could not find enough insects to feed it.
2. Then we found that the little bird liked dog food.
3. It also liked little bits of cooked egg yolk.
4. We even made some worms out of hamburger meat.

Review (P. 23)

A.
1. X
2. S
3. S
4. X

B.
1. Did Joseph fly to Boston?
2. interrogative
3. interrogative
4. Is taking the train slower?

C.
1. imperative
2. imperative
3. imperative
4. exclamatory
5. exclamatory

D. Students should circle the words in bold.
1. My cousin **Lee plays** hockey for the Hawks.
2. **He practices** early every morning.
3. Hockey **players love** the sport.
4. **They play** even in the coldest weather.
5. The **game** of hockey **has** very dedicated players and fans.
6. **Players skate** madly around the rink.

Review (P. 24)

E.
1. compound
2. simple
3. simple
4. compound

F. Sentences may vary. Suggested:

Hank got up early. He reviewed his notes again. So, the test today would be easy for him.

G. Andrea likes baked chicken.

H. Sentences may vary. Suggested:
1. I was tired of moving.
2. My family had moved four times in the past three years.
3. Leaving my friends was always the hardest.
4. It's not easy to start over and make new ones.
5. Now we can stay put in a town that I like.

I. Sentences will vary.

Using What You've Learned (P. 25)

A.
1. sentence
2. Sentences will vary.
3. Sentences will vary.
4. sentence

B. The stripes on it stand for the first thirteen colonies. The stars represent the fifty states. The colors have a meaning, too. White means freedom from wrong. Red stands for courage. Blue stands for fairness. Everything on the flag has a meaning.

1. How much do you know about the U.S. flag?
2. What do you think the stars stand for?
3. Did you know that?

C. 1. Did Jetta run to the grocery store?
2. Did she buy bread and milk?
3. Did she stop at the park?
4. Was Jetta surprised at how long she was gone?

D. Sentences will vary.

Using What You've Learned (P. 26)

E. Fingerprints can prove who a person is. A light powder is used so fingerprints can be seen. Each person's fingerprints are different from anyone else's fingerprints. Even the fingerprints of twins are different. A person's fingerprints stay the same as he or she grows older.

1. Fingerprints	can prove
2. powder	is used
3. fingerprints	are
4. fingerprints	are
5. fingerprints	stay

F. Oranges are grown in Florida, and grapefruit are also grown there. Other fruits grow in Florida, but citrus fruit is still the main crop.
1. The main product of Florida is citrus fruit.
2. Citrus fruit needs warm weather to grow.
3. Many vegetables are also grown in Florida.

G. Sentences may vary. Suggested:
Flies are interesting insects. The eyes of a fly have up to 400 parts. They really see only motion and light. A fly has six legs and six feet. Each foot has a pair of claws.

Unit 3 Grammar and Usage

Lesson 19, Nouns (P. 27)

A. 1. Mrs. Smith has a big job ahead.
2. She needs to plan a picnic for her family.
3. Mrs. Smith must find a big park.
4. The family always enjoys the picnic.
5. It is a big event every year.
6. Mr. Smith is planning some games.
7. He will set up a net for volleyball.
8. Margie will make the hamburgers.
9. Mrs. Smith finally picked Riverview Park.
10. The park is on the Mississippi River.

B.

1. thing	8. person
2. person	9. place
3. person	10. person
4. place	11. place
5. person	12. thing
6. thing	13. person
7. place	

Lesson 20, Proper and Common Nouns (P. 28)

A.

1. cousin, holidays	4. stories
2. country	5. year
3. cousin, visitor	

B. 1. Dr. Alvarado, New York
2. Parkside Hospital
3. September
4. Roosevelt University; Queens, New York
5. United States

C. Answers will vary.

Lesson 21, Singular and Plural Nouns (P. 29)

A.

1. S; porches	8. P; half
2. S; chairs	9. S; pencils
3. P; girl	10. S; alleys
4. S; wives	11. P; leaf
5. P; fly	12. S; pouches
6. S; skies	13. P; inch
7. P; fox	14. S; shelves

B. Students should circle the words in bold.

1. plural	**programs**
2. singular	**hour**
3. singular	**time**
4. singular	**family**
5. plural	**magazines**
6. singular	**show**

Lesson 22, Singular Possessive Nouns (P. 30)

A.

1. my aunt's house	4. my brother's bicycle
2. my cousin's dog	5. the cook's apron
3. my friend's books	

B.

1. Jerry's	4. automobile's
2. officer's	5. city's
3. thief's	

C.

1. store's	3. clerk's	5. man's
2. Lisa's	4. bag's	

Lesson 23, Plural Possessive Nouns (P. 31)

A.

1. sisters'	4. members'
2. uniforms'	5. instruments'
3. parents'	

B.

1. Farmers'	4. sheep's
2. children's	5. cows'
3. ponds'	6. barns'

Lesson 24, Action Verbs (P. 32)

A.

1. jumped	10. yawned
2. leaped	11. chewed
3. snapped	12. snarled
4. spun	13. teased
5. arched	14. pulled
6. pulled	15. snapped
7. danced	16. shot
8. howled	17. bounded
9. licked	18. scrambled

B. Predicates will vary.

Lesson 25, Linking Verbs (P. 33)

A. Linking verbs may vary. Suggested:

1. is	**5.** seem
2. grow	**6.** taste
3. smells	**7.** sound
4. look	**8.** become

B.

1. L	**5.** L
3. L	**6.** L

Lesson 26, Helping Verbs (P. 34)

Students should circle the words in bold.

1. had wanted	**11. has** gone
2. had planned	**12. had** told
3. has gone	**13. was** going
4. were waiting	**14. had** planned
5. was raking	**15. am** going
6. were looking	**16. have** seen
7. couldn't find	**17. are** taking
8. were forced	**18. is** meeting
9. was given	**19. is** riding
10. is going	**20. are** looking

Lesson 27, Verb Tenses (P. 35)

A.

1. past	**7.** future
2. past	**8.** present
3. present	**9.** future
4. future	**10.** future
5. present	**11.** future
6. past	

B. Verbs will vary.

Lesson 28, Regular Verbs (P. 36)

A.

1. looked	**6.** crushed
2. gasped	**7.** scratched
3. settled	**8.** headed
4. stepped	**9.** changed
5. hurried	**10.** dropped

B.
1. sailed the boat
2. steered a straight course
3. carried the sail
4. enjoyed the fresh air and sunshine

Lesson 29, Irregular Verbs (P. 37)

A.

1. went	**10.** flew
2. left	**11.** said
3. took	**12.** began
4. knew	**13.** wrote
5. grew	**14.** broke
6. saw	**15.** threw
7. gave	**16.** chose
8. sat	**17.** fell
9. came	**18.** ran

Lesson 30, Making Subjects and Verbs Agree (P. 38)

1. eat; plural	**10.** acts; singular
2. lives; singular	**11.** drop; plural
3. fly; plural	**12.** watches; singular
4. feeds; singular	**13.** spread; plural
5. scratch; plural	**14.** kills; singular
6. cause; plural	**15.** lose; plural
7. destroys; singular	**16.** needs; singular
8. fight; plural	**17.** help; plural
9. slows; singular	

Lesson 31, Subjects and Linking Verbs (P. 39)

A. Answers may vary. Suggested:
1. was
2. was
3. were
4. is
5. are
6. are
7. is
8. is

B. Answers may vary. Suggested:
1. There are
2. There were
3. There is
4. There are
5. There are
6. There is
7. There are
8. There is

Lesson 32, Subject Pronouns (P. 40)

A.

1. She	**5.** We
2. It	**6.** I
3. They	**7.** He
4. You	**8.** I

B.

1. I	**5.** They
2. We	**6.** you
3. He	**7.** She
4. It	**8.** I

C. Sentences will vary.

Lesson 33, Object Pronouns (P. 41)

A.

1. it	**5.** them
2. us	**6.** you
3. me	**7.** him
4. us	**8.** me

B.

1. me	**5.** them
2. him	**6.** them
3. it	**7.** her
4. us	**8.** them

C. Sentences will vary.

Lesson 34, Using Pronouns (P. 42)

1. We	**6.** He
2. They	**7.** him
3. It	**8.** she
4. them	**9.** her
5. us	**10.** us

Lesson 35, Possessive Pronouns (P. 43)

1. My
2. our
3. Its
4. My or Our
5. his
6. his
7. her
8. our
9. Your or My
10. your or my
11. their
12. his or our
13. her
14. her
15. Their, Her, or Its
16. our
17. its, his, or her
18. my or our
19. Its
20. your

Lesson 36, Adjectives (P. 44)

A. 1. big, tiny
2. sharp, bright
3. scared, small
4. speeding, wet
5. tired, dark
6. damp, big
7. little, wide

B. Answers may vary. Suggested:
Line 1. Many, beautiful
Line 2. sparkling
Line 3. dark; Wild
Line 4. green; Gentle
Line 5. fierce
Line 1. young or strong; wooden or shaky
Line 2. strong or soft; thick
Line 3. best or young; shaky or wooden
Line 4. six, red; soft
Line 5. bare

Lesson 37, Adjectives That Compare (P. 45)

A. 1. smallest
2. smaller
3. cutest
4. funnier
5. whitest
6. longest
7. naughtiest
8. harder
9. later
10. busier
11. happiest
12. biggest

B. 1. lighter
2. darkest
3. straighter
4. wildest
5. longer
6. shortest
7. longer
8. warmer
9. colder
10. coldest

Lesson 38, Adverbs (P. 46)

A. 1. widely, cheerfully
2. Yesterday, calmly
3. quickly, loudly
4. Later, quietly

B. 1. quietly, how
2. softly, how
3. Later; when
4. there, where

C. Answers may vary. Suggested:
1. quickly
2. there
3. Suddenly
4. brightly
5. anxiously
6. slowly
7. totally
8. hopelessly
9. quietly

Lesson 39, Adverbs That Compare (P. 47)

A. 1. faster
2. later
3. latest
4. sooner
5. most carefully
6. harder

B. 1. later
2. most quietly or quietest
3. more loudly or louder
4. more peacefully
5. nearest
6. more slowly or slower
7. sooner
8. more carefully

Lesson 40, Using Words Correctly (P. 48)

A. 1. well, good
2. well
3. good
4. well
5. well
6. good
7. well
8. good
9. good
10. well
11. good

B. 1. any
2. any
3. nothing
4. ever
5. any
6. anything
7. anybody

Lesson 41, Using Other Words Correctly (P. 49)

A. 1. those
2. them
3. them, them
4. those
5. them, those
6. them
7. those
8. those

B. 1. don't
2. doesn't
3. doesn't
4. doesn't
5. don't, doesn't
6. doesn't
7. don't
8. don't

Review (P. 50)

A. Students should circle the words in bold and box the words in italics.
1. Mark, **car**
2. **town**, Chester
3. Jan, **farm**
4. **horse**, Bullet
5. Bullet, *Jan's,* **pet**
6. **horse, dogs, burro**
7. **burro**, All Ears, ***horse's***, **barn**
8. ***dogs'***, **home**, **porch**

B. 1. H
2. A
3. H
4. L
5. H
6. L
7. A
8. A

C. 1. received
2. will decide
3. choose
4. went
5. likes
6. grew

Review (P. 51)

D. 1. are
2. There are
3. follow
4. used
5. was
6. There were
7. were
8. gave
9. said
10. are, added

E. 1. She, him
2. She, it
3. Her
4. He, it, it
5. She, he
6. They, their
7. She
8. he, it
9. his
10. she, he

F. Students should circle the words in bold.
1. adjective; **movie**
2. adjective; **dazzling**
3. adjective; **wonderful**
4. adjective; **bigger**
5. adverb; **quickly**
6. adverb; **Later**
7. adverb; **harder**
8. adjective; **good**

Using What You've Learned (P. 52)

A. 1.

Common	Proper
house	Marty
idea	Charleston
history	Mr. Bremmer
people	
place	
door	

2. As he stood outside the old house, Marty wondered if this was a good idea. He wanted to go in, but the history of the house stopped him. All of the people in Charleston knew of Mr. Bremmer and this place. Marty started to walk toward the door. He still wondered if he should.

B. Students should circle the words in bold.
1. Some jobs **are** not worth the money.
2. We **agree** with that.
3. Whoever **watches** this place must be brave.
4. Marty **is** not sure that he **is** brave enough.

Using What You've Learned (P. 53)

C. Marty got up his nerve and walked to the house. The front of it was dark. There were faces carved in the stone. They looked mean. "Those/They are strange," he thought. They scared him. "Oh well, here I go," he said to himself.

D. Answers may vary. Suggested:
1. rusty, slowly
2. scariest, ever
3. noisy, quieter
4. shaky, barely
5. brighter, strangely

E. **Line 1.** doesn't
Line 2. Those
Line 3. don't; ever
Line 4. anything
Line 5. well
Line 6. ever

Unit 4 Capitalization and Punctuation

Lesson 42, Names of People and Pets (P. 54)

1. Uncle George got up early today.
2. He and Aunt Beth had a special job to do.
3. Uncle George and Aunt Beth were going to the animal shelter.
4. They wanted to find a puppy for Susan and Michael.
5. Uncle George and Aunt Beth thought a small dog would be nice.
6. But Susan and Michael wanted a big dog.
7. Uncle George saw a cute kitten named Mittens.
8. In the very last cage, they saw Sasha.
9. Uncle George and Aunt Beth loved her at once.
10. When Sasha ran circles around Michael, he loved her, too.

Lesson 43, Names of Places and Things (P. 55)

A. 1. Our family will spend Memorial Day in Washington.
2. We hope to see the White House and the Washington Monument.
3. We also want to see the Smithsonian Institution.
4. The Potomac River forms a border between Washington and Virginia.
5. The Lincoln Memorial is amazing to see at night.
6. The Vietnam Memorial gets many visitors.
7. There are many amazing sights in Washington.

B. Answers will vary.

Lesson 44, Capitalizing Titles (P. 56)

A. 1. Doctor William H. Black
2. Judge Rosa Allen
3. A Wrinkle in Time
4. Captain William Faircroft
5. The President of the United States
6. Doctor Laurie C. Bell
7. Attack of the Monster Plants
8. Major Carol Gates
9. Owls in the Family
10. My Side of the Mountain

B. 1. Mr. Thomas's
2. Judge George King
3. Judge King; Judge Claire Booth; Life in the Courts
4. Ms. Dias; Life in the Courts; Judge Booth
5. A Judge's Story; Raymond Field

Lesson 45, Capitalizing Abbreviations (P. 57)

A. **1.** Tues.
2. Wed.
3. Thurs.
4. Fri.
5. Sat.
6. Sun.
7. Jan.
8. Nov.
9. Sept.
10. Aug.
11. Oct.
12. Dec.

B. **1.** The conference is planned for Aug. 12.
2. It will be held in Wm. Taft Park.
3. George W. Bush will be there.
4. Our mayor, Ms. Foster, was pleased he could come.
5. Police Chief E. S. Rodriguez will introduce him.
6. Many people want to hear Mr. Bush speak.
7. They want to know how he likes life away from Washington, D.C.

Lesson 46, Parts of a Letter (P. 58)

7216 melvin street
houston, tx 77040
october 23, 1994

dear fred,
I am doing a report on farm life. Do you have any information you can send me? My report must be turned in three weeks from today. I can really use any help you can give me. Pictures and facts would be helpful. The names of some books I could find at the library would also help a lot.

your friend,
jesse

---

820 w. state st.
lockhart, al 36455
october 29, 1994

dear jesse,
I'll be glad to help with your report. Better yet, why don't you come and visit? Call and let me know if you are coming. The library here serves all of alabama. I know we could find all the information you need.

your friend,
fred

Lesson 47, Sentences (P. 59)

A. Students should circle the letters in bold.
1. **i** am going to ride my bike to the store.
2. **w**here is my bike?
3. **i**t is always in the garage by the hose.
4. **c**ould it be on the back porch?
5. **i**'ll ask Joanne if she has seen it.
6. **s**he said it was in the garage this morning.
7. **o**h, no, someone has stolen my bike!
8. **w**hat should I do now?
9. **w**ho could have taken it?

B. **1.** I'll call the police about my bike.
2. Hurry, hurry, answer the phone!
3. Hello, is this the police station?
4. Yes, what can we do for you?
5. You must help me catch a bike thief.
6. How do you know your bike wasn't borrowed?

Lesson 48, Using Commas in Sentences (P. 60)

1. I called Juan, Janet, and Karen last Saturday.
2. Yes, they wanted to have a picnic.
3. Juan packed a lunch, and Karen brought a backpack.
4. Well, we were finally ready to go.
5. Yes, we found a perfect place by the beach.
6. We played volleyball, swam, and hiked.
7. It was a great picnic, and there were no ants around.
8. We collected shells, driftwood, and pebbles.
9. Juan cleaned up the garbage, and Karen packed the leftovers.
10. We sang, laughed, and read.

Lesson 49, Using Commas in Other Sentences (P. 61)

A. **1.** Our neighbor, Buddy Rush, is gone.
2. Mr. Rush, his father, said he doesn't know where Buddy is.
3. Danny, did Buddy talk about going somewhere?
4. This seems very strange to me, Tim.
5. Chief Carter, our sheriff, thinks so, too.
6. Buddy, where are you?
7. Danny, don't you remember what I told you?
8. What should we do now, Chief Carter?

B. **1.** X Someone is talking to Craig.
2. X Someone is talking to Lydia.
3. X Mrs. Hicks is our neighbor.
4. X Someone is talking to Carrie.
5. X Anna is my dog.

Lesson 50, Using Commas in Letters (P. 62)

A.

422 W. South St.
Dallas, TX 72843
November 12, 1994

Dear Mark,
Thank you for coming to my party. It was fun having you there. I also want to thank you for the great sweatshirt. It fits fine, and I really like it.

Your friend,
Theresa

8200 Columbus Ave.
Dallas, TX 72844
November 16, 1994

Dear Theresa,
Don't forget about the trip to the museum on Saturday. See you there.

Sincerely,
Mark

B. 1. 321 Pebble Beach Drive
Jacksonville, FL 32211
November 17, 1994

2. 101 Main St.
Oakland, CA 10032
July 10, 1994

C. 1. Dear Juana,
2. Sincerely yours,
3. Your friend,
4. Dear Grandmother,
5. Your grandson,
6. Hi, Scott,

Lesson 51, Using Quotation Marks (P. 63)

1. "Do you want to talk about the interesting places we each visited this summer?" asked Ms. Chen.
2. "My sister and I visited my aunt in Nome, Alaska," said James. Or: James said, "My sister...Alaska."
3. "We flew to Quebec to see our grandmother," said Jenny. Or: Jenny said, "We flew...grandmother."
4. "We went to Arizona and saw the Grand Canyon," said Richard. Or: Richard said, "We went...Grand Canyon."

Lesson 52, More About Quotation Marks (P. 64)

1. "Well," said Mike, "Dot is just getting over a strange accident."
2. "What happened?" asked Susan.
3. "A thought struck her," said Mike.
4. Jake asked, "Why did you throw the alarm clock out the window?"
5. "Because," said Joan, "I wanted to see time fly."
6. "What did one wall say to another?" asked Bonnie.
7. "I'll meet you at the corner," answered David.
8. "What gets wetter," Carlos asked, "the more you dry?"
9. "A towel does," said Angie.
10. Mother said, "Are your feet dirty?"
11. "Yes," replied Bobby, "but don't worry because I have my shoes on."
12. Maria asked, "How can you tell when an ice cube is nervous?"
13. "It breaks out," said Bill, "in a cold sweat."
14. Anna asked, "What is black-and-white and red all over?"
15. "It's a blushing zebra," said Jake.
16. "What did the rug say to the floor?" asked Mike.
17. "Don't move," replied Bonnie, "because I've got you covered."
18. Joan asked, "Why do sponges do a good job?"
19. "They become absorbed in their work," said Carlos.
20. Angie asked, "Why is a pencil like a riddle?"
21. "Because," said Maria, "it's no good without a point."

Lesson 53, Apostrophes in Contractions (P. 65)

A.

1. she will	**4.** I will
2. We are	**5.** She is
3. they will	**6.** We had

B.

1. It's;	we're	**4.** didn't	should've
2. You're;	we've	**5.** I'll;	we'll
3. I'm;	they'll	**6.** We're;	I'm

Lesson 54, Apostrophes to Show Possession (P. 66)

A. 1. brother's
2. car's
3. Dad's
4. sisters'
5. family's
6. friends'

B. 1. We all liked Jennifer's story the best.
2. The story's setting was an old castle.
3. There was a prison in the castle's basement.
4. The students' attention was on Jennifer as she read.
5. A cruel man lived in the castle's tower.
6. The cruel man's children weren't allowed to play.

Review (P. 67)

A. Students should circle the letters in bold.
1. **m**arjorie took her horse, **b**laze, out for a ride.
2. **s**he rode through **p**laceville to the **m**iller house.
3. **m**r. **m**iller's mother, **j**udge **m**iller, was on the **s**upreme **c**ourt.
4. **j**udge **m**iller served from **s**ept. 1960 to **a**ug. 1990.
5. **h**er record was well-known in **w**ashington, **d**. **c**.
6. **s**enator **h**iggins often went to her for advice.
7. **m**arjorie and her friends loved to hear **j**udge **m**iller talk about her experiences.

B.

5780 W. Natchez
Miles, VT 05857
December 10, 1994

Dear Pam,

It's been a long time since my last letter. How are you? Everything is fine here, but I really miss having you as a neighbor. Amy, our new neighbor, is nice. She goes to Taft School, and she is in my class. No, she will never replace you as my best friend. Oh, I almost forgot! Mrs. Tandy said, "Tell Pam hello for me." We all miss you a lot. Do you still think you can visit this summer?

Your friend,
Delia

C. 1. "Henry, stand by the door for a minute," said Scott.
2. "What for?" asked Henry.
3. "I want you to hold the door," answered Scott, "while I bring in this table."
4. Henry asked, "Are you going to carry that by yourself?"
5. "It's not very heavy," said Scott.
6. "What are you going to do with it?" asked Henry.
7. "We need it for the kitchen," said Scott.

Review (P. 68)

D. 1. "Well, it's time to get to work," said Lisa.
2. Lisa walked out of the room, and Jeremy followed her.
3. Lisa pointed to the trash can.
4. "What a mess!" Jeremy cried.
5. "Your dog did this," said Lisa.
6. "Oh, so now Peanut's all mine," said Jeremy.
7. "Yes, when he's bad, he's yours," said Lisa.
8. They laughed and cleaned up the trash together.

E. 1. I'll see what needs to be done with dinner's leftovers.
2. I think they're cool enough to put on the refrigerator's shelf.
3. Dan hopes we're not going to have that for tomorrow's lunch.
4. He doesn't think that his sister's daughters will eat it.
5. He's wrong; cold pizza is his nieces' favorite food.
6. They'll be happy with this lunch's surprise.

Using What You've Learned (P. 69)

A. Students should circle the letters in bold.

miriam **s**tone, WBZI's top reporter, woke up early. **s**he said, "I have plenty of time to get ready." **s**he thought of the letter she received yesterday:

920 **s**. **l**ake **st**.
kansas **c**ity, **mo** 43210
april 1, 1994

dear **m**iriam,
if you want a really exciting story, meet me at the **j**.**m**. **b**anister **l**ibrary at ten o'clock tomorrow morning. I'm sure your station's newsroom will want this story.

yours truly,
A Fan

she asked herself what it could be. **m**iriam dressed, ate breakfast, got her notebook, and headed for the library. **i**t was not far, and soon she was there.

suddenly, a short woman in a dark dress walked up and said, "I wrote the letter." **s**he said, "**y**ou must hear my story."

"**m**y name is **j**uanita," she said. "I've been tricked by a gang of crooks. **i** need your help."

miriam said, "**t**ell me your story, and I'll see what I can do."

juanita told **m**iriam of a man named **g**eneral **j**.**c**. **c**ook who said he worked for the **u**nited **s**tates **a**rmy. **h**e told her he needed a key to all the safety boxes in the bank where she worked. "**y**es," she said, "**i**t was strange, but he said it was for the country." **n**ow all of the boxes had been robbed, and she was sure it was **g**eneral **c**ook's work.

miriam was excited about the story. "**n**ow," said **m**iriam, "tell me everything you can remember about **g**eneral **j**.**c**. **c**ook."

"**w**ow, what a story!" **m**iriam said excitedly.

Using What You've Learned (P. 70)

B.

420 Station St.
Park Ridge, IL 60010
April 3, 1994

Dear Mr. Thompson,

I appreciate the time you spent with me Tuesday. I learned a great deal about Thompson's Freight Lines, and I am sure that I would do a good job for your company. I have two years of experience in shipping goods around the world.

It was a pleasure to meet you and speak with you. What a surprise to learn that you know my Uncle Joe so well! He speaks very highly of you and your company.

Thank you again for seeing me. I'll call you in a few days.

Yours truly,
Wayne S. Carver

Unit 5 Composition

Lesson 55, Writing Sentences (P. 71)

1. a. yes; Nora
b. yes; needed a hobby
c. yes; yes

2. a. yes; Nora
b. no; there isn't one
c. no; no

3. a. no; there isn't one
b. yes; will do a family history
c. no; no

4. a. yes; Nora
b. yes; began planning
c. yes; yes

5. a. no; there isn't one
b. yes; asked questions
c. no; no

Lesson 56, Writing Topic Sentences (P. 72)

A. Nora decided that she needed a hobby.

B. To get the information she needed, Nora would have to ask many questions. She thought about the kinds of questions she would ask. She wanted to make sure that she didn't forget any questions. So Nora wrote down a list of questions that she would ask each person. Next, she made copies of the list. She put one person's name at the top of each copy. Then she was ready to talk to people.

Lesson 57, Writing Supporting Details (P. 73)

Students should cross out sentences 4, 5, and 8.

Nora was ready to begin her history. First, she put her questions into a notebook. She made sure she had pens and extra paper. Then Nora called Grandpa Casey and asked when she could come and talk to him. She also called Grandpa Vargas. Both of her grandfathers were glad to help with the family history.

Lesson 58, Time Order in Paragraphs (P. 74)

Sentence order: 3, 4, 9, 7, 8, 1, 6, 2, 5, and 10

Lesson 59, Writing a Conversation (P. 75)

Paragraphs may vary. Suggested:

Nora asked, "What was it like when you were growing up?"

"I will tell you about my boyhood in Mexico," said Grandpa Vargas.

"My father raised sheep. I used to watch the flock of sheep," said Grandpa Vargas.

"It was not an easy job because wolves were always nearby," he said.

Nora said, "Please tell me about the wolves."

Lesson 60, Topic and Audience (P. 76)

A. **1.** adult
2. child
3. teenager
4. adult
5. child
6. teenager
7. teenager
8. child
9. adult
10. child
11. adult

B. Topics and audiences will vary.

Lesson 61, Planning an Outline (P. 77)

Outlines will vary.

Lesson 62, A Narrative Paragraph (P. 78)

1. Topic Sentence: "Ah," said Grandpa, "my meeting with the wolf was very exciting."
Time order words: Then, Next, Finally, Afterward

2. Answers may vary.
They had just arrived at the meadow.
The sheep and Blanco were unsettled.
Blanco leaped on a sheep's back and raced across the flock.
The wolf attacked.
Blanco fought the wolf.
Grandpa yelled and swung the stick at the wolf.
The wolf left.
Grandpa and Blanco felt proud.

Lesson 63, Writing a Narrative Paragraph (P. 79)

Topics, topic sentences, and paragraphs will vary.

Review (P. 80)

A. **1.** sentence
2. She (Nora) could listen for hours.
3. sentence
4. She (Nora) wished her life was that interesting.

B. Students should underline: Nora wanted to make a lasting history of her family.

C. Students should cross out sentence 4.

Nora planned her recorded history. She read through her list of questions. Then she thought about how much time each would take to answer. Next, she went shopping for blank tapes. Finally, she was ready to let her grandfathers tell their stories.

Review (P. 81)

D. Conversations may vary. Suggested:

Nora asked, "How did you get to the United States, Grandpa Casey?"
"I came to Boston from Ireland by ship," said Grandpa Casey.
"Where is your favorite place?" asked Nora.
Grandpa Casey said, "I like it where I am right now."

E. **Statement:** Writing a narrative paragraph
I. Choose a topic
II. Write a topic sentence
III. Write information about the topic
A. Add supporting details
B. Use time order words

F. Students should circle the words in bold.

Grandpa's twin brothers played tricks on people. **First**, they'd dress exactly alike. **Then** they'd both answer when people said one of their names. **Finally**, they'd look at each other and laugh.

Using What You've Learned (P. 82)

A. Topics will vary.

B. Statements will vary.

C. Outlines will vary.

Using What You've Learned (P. 83)

D. Topic sentences will vary.

E. Paragraphs will vary.

Unit 6 Study Skills

Lesson 64, Alphabetical Order (P. 84)

1. 3, 7, 1, 6, 5, 2, 8, 4
2. 6, 1, 7, 4, 2, 5, 8, 9, 3
3. 7, 6, 1, 8, 3, 2, 4, 5
4. 2, 8, 1, 6, 9, 4, 3, 5, 7
5. 1, 4, 8, 2, 6, 3, 5, 7
6. 9, 6, 3, 2, 7, 8, 4, 1, 5

Lesson 65, Dictionary: Guide Words (P. 85)

A. Students should circle the following words:
1. anxious
amount
arrest
alive
also
ant
allow
2. fourth
flower
fog
fly
flame
flew
flight
3. side
shawl
seventeen
sink
settle
sign
shelter

B. **1.** lake / lead
lake
lamp
lap
last
late
lawn
lead

2. pack / pat
pack
pad
page
palm
pan
pass
pat

Lesson 66, Dictionary: Pronunciation (P. 86)

A. **1.** girl
2. lowly
3. write
4. trout
5. glide
6. huge
7. gallop
8. hug
9. vanish

B. **1.** word
2. dictionary
3. guide
4. found
5. respelling

Lesson 67, Dictionary: Definitions (P. 87)

A. **1.** noun
2. adjective
3. verb
4. folktale, follower, folly
5. Sentences will vary.

B. Sentences will vary.

Lesson 68, Dictionary: Multiple Meanings (P. 88)

A. **1.** 3; 3; 3
2. 2; 5

B. **1.** 1
2. 2
3. 1
4. 1
5. 3

Lesson 69, Using an Encyclopedia (P. 89)

A. **1.** vitamins
2. to keep your body healthy
3. to get all the vitamins your body needs
4. during periods of rapid growth, during stress, and while recovering from an illness
5. minerals
6. they both are needed by the body for good health
7. no

Lesson 69, Using an Encyclopedia (P. 90)

B. **1.** Mandela
2. food
3. United
4. oceans
5. Thatcher
6. United
7. games
8. dogs

C. **1.** 9
2. 2
3. 16
4. 16
5. 13
6. 2
7. 21
8. 19

Lesson 70, Parts of a Book (P. 91)

1. Language Exercises, Level D
2. page 27
3. 30, 31, 65, 66, 68, 69, 70, 103
4. 1995
5. Saranna Moeller, Betty Jones, and Cynthia T. Strauch
6. 6
7. 84
8. 108
9. 46, 47, 51, 101
10. Lesson 34, Using Pronouns
11. 32, 50, 100
12. Steck-Vaughn Company
13. Lesson 63, Writing a Narrative Paragraph

Review (P. 92)

A. fruit
morning
onion
pizza
ran
wag

B. **1.** debt, deck — defend, degree
2. demand, den — depend, design

C. **1.** need
2. dictionary
3. say
4. sentence

D. **1.** verb
2. ours
3. chuck

Review (P. 93)

E. **1.** Mark Twain
2. 1910
3. The Adventures of Huckleberry Finn
4. Hannibal, Missouri
5. It is his real name.

F. **1.** computers, 1
2. Einstein, 2
3. Amazon, 1
4. Norway, 5
5. Romania, 6
6. eagles, 2

G. **1.** title page
2. title page
3. index
4. copyright page
5. table of contents
6. copyright page

Using What You've Learned (P. 94)

A. Answers will vary.

B. **1.** noun
2. Definitions will vary.
3. Sentences will vary.
4. Respellings will vary.

Using What You've Learned (P. 95)

C. Guide words and respellings will vary.

1. ache	**6.** howl
2. ancient	**7.** magician
3. blizzard	**8.** remind
4. disease	**9.** scent
5. helpful	**10.** venture

D. Answers will vary.

Final Reviews

Final Review, Unit 1 (P. 96)

1. smiled, grinned
2. ran, dashed
3. spoke, talked

1. wrong
2. remembered
3. sad

1. hear	**6.** there
2. too	**7.** write
3. It's	**8.** Its, here
4. they're	**9.** their
5. two, right	**10.** too, to

1. take up a weapon
2. noise a dog makes
3. ran quickly

Final Review, Unit 1 (P. 97)

1. P	**4.** S
2. P	**5.** P
3. S	

1. straw, berries
2. rattle, snake
3. sand, paper

1. it's	**3.** I'm
2. couldn't	**4.** won't
3. they'll	

Students should circle the words in bold.

Many people think he's gone to the **seashore**. But they're wrong. He'd rather go to his **mountaintop hideaway**. He'll stay there until **somebody** gets worried. Then they'll remember and call him there. He won't let **anything** but an emergency make him come back until he's ready!

Final Review, Unit 2 (P. 98)

1. X	**4.** S	**7.** S
2. X	**5.** X	**8.** X
3. S	**6.** S	

1. interrogative
2. exclamatory
3. imperative
4. declarative
5. interrogative
6. declarative
7. declarative
8. exclamatory

1. predicate
2. subject
3. predicate
4. subject

Students should circle the words in bold.

1. For years **factories** dumped wastes into lakes and rivers.
2. Some waste **materials** cause no harm.
3. Other **waste** poisoned the water.
4. Today many **factories** protect the water from wastes.

Final Review, Unit 2 (P. 99)

1. compound
2. simple
3. simple
4. compound
5. simple
6. compound

Answers may vary. Suggested:

1. Jessie went fishing, and Ted went swimming.
2. Yesterday was cold, but today is a rainy, gray day.
3. Canada and the United States are neighbors, and they are friends.

Paragraphs may vary. Suggested:

My grandmother was a pioneer. She traveled by wagon train to Missouri. When she turned 12, she decided she wanted to ride a horse. Her father told her she couldn't do that in a skirt. So she had her mother make her some pants. She wanted to be on her own. She wanted more freedom. She kept a diary, and I've read it all. That's how I know.

Final Review, Unit 3 (P. 100)

Students should circle the words in bold.

1. Sally sat next to the **window.**
2. It was a wonderful **morning** in June.
3. Warm **mornings** in California are very beautiful.

1. dog's
2. puppies'
3. dogs
4. tails

1. A
2. A
3. H
4. A
5. H
6. L

1. present
2. future
3. past

1. plural, are
2. plural, read
3. singular, is
4. singular, likes

Final Review, Unit 3 (P. 101)

1. P; Her job is park ranger.
2. S; She loves spending every day in the forest.
3. O; Her favorite thing is walking among them.
4. P; She really likes it when their leaves change.
5. P; Ed sometimes brings his camera to take pictures.
6. P; Its pictures are clear and sharp.

1. adverb
2. adjective
3. adjective
4. adjective
5. adverb
6. adverb

1. don't
2. ever
3. good
4. them
5. doesn't
6. those
7. well

Final Review, Unit 4 (P. 102)

328 N. State St.
New York, NY 10010
January 2, 1994

Dear Dr. Turner,

I want to thank you for your kindness to Tootsie, my pet bird. My friend, Jack, said, "No one knows how to cure birds. They're different from other types of pets. You shouldn't waste your money." Can you believe that? I didn't agree with Jack, so I brought Tootsie to your office. Thanks to you, Tootsie is fine again.

Sincerely,
Juan Gomez

Final Review, Unit 4 (P. 103)

1. "Our next topic," said Mr. Lopez, "will be the fall of the Roman Empire."
2. "Hurry and get out of there!" cried Louis.
3. Ted, please don't ask me to do that.
4. "Has the jury reached a verdict?" asked Judge Mallory.
5. Eric said, "I'll be the first to tell you if you're right."
6. Well, I guess it's all right.
7. We spent the day swimming, hiking, and having a picnic.

1. Didn't you see the look on Dean's face?
2. It's pretty clear he doesn't like our plan.
3. He hasn't said anything at all about Frank's idea.
4. We're going to have to make up our minds soon.
5. The men's ideas are different from ours.
6. Everyone's ideas should be considered.

Final Review, Unit 5 (P. 104)

Students should circle the words in bold.

Forests grow in a cycle. **First**, the strongest trees grow very large. **Then** the other trees cannot get enough sunlight. Weaker trees either stay short or die. **Afterward**, new growth begins.

Conversations will vary. Suggested:

"Chris, did you understand the movie?" asked Bob.
"I'm not sure," Chris said. "I thought I did at first, but then I got confused."
"I did, too," said Bob.
"What did you think of it, Bob?" asked Chris.
Bob said, "I liked it, but I wondered about the ending."
Chris said, "The writer was probably as confused as we were!"

Final Review, Unit 5 (P. 105)

Statement: Cowboys in the Old West

I. Equipment
  A. Saddle and bridle
  B. Gun and rope
II. Clothing

Paragraphs may vary. Suggested:

Judy had planned her day well. Tonight she would invite her parents over for dinner. First, she cleaned her entire house. She chose the clothes she would wear. Next, she went to the florist and bought a blue glass vase. Then she bought a beautiful bunch of flowers. She took the vase and flowers back home and put them on the table. After that, she went shopping for a special meal. Finally, she prepared the meal and waited for her parents to arrive.

Final Review, Unit 6 (P. 106)

rich / rock
1. rich
2. right
3. rinse
4. rob
5. rock

baby / bat
1. baby
2. back
3. ball
4. base
5. bat

Respellings will vary.

1. adjective
2. 5
3. adjective, verb
4. **a.** verb, 1
   b. adjective, 2
   c. adjective, 1

Final Review, Unit 6 (P. 107)

1. the elbow
2. a joint between the upper and lower arm
3. it allows the arm to bend, twist, and turn
4. arm and wrist
5. no, only arm is mentioned

1. sea, 7
2. Hong, 3
3. nursing, 5
4. fly, 2
5. Keller, 4
6. aluminum, 1
7. vampires, 8
8. horses, 3
9. Shakespeare, 7
10. boomerangs, 1
11. instruments, 3
12. New, 5

1. table of contents
2. index
3. title page
4. copyright page

Tests

TEST: Unit 1, Pages 21–22, Teacher's Guide

1. B	**12.** A	**23.** A
2. B	**13.** D	**24.** D
3. A	**14.** C	**25.** D
4. D	**15.** C	**26.** B
5. A	**16.** D	**27.** A
6. C	**17.** A	**28.** B
7. B	**18.** C	**29.** B
8. D	**19.** D	**30.** B
9. C	**20.** B	**31.** D
10. B	**21.** C	**32.** D
11. B	**22.** B	**33.** C

TEST: Unit 2, Pages 23–24, Teacher's Guide

1. D	**13.** D
2. B	**14.** B
3. A	**15.** C
4. D	**16.** C
5. B	**17.** B
6. D	**18.** D
7. C	**19.** B
8. A	**20.** C
9. C	**21.** B
10. A	**22.** C
11. C	
12. D	

TEST: Unit 3, Pages 25–26, Teacher's Guide

1. C	**11.** A	**21.** B
2. D	**12.** D	**22.** A
3. C	**13.** A	**23.** C
4. A	**14.** C	**24.** C
5. D	**15.** B	**25.** D
6. D	**16.** D	**26.** C
7. B	**17.** C	**27.** A
8. A	**18.** B	**28.** C
9. B	**19.** C	
10. A	**20.** D	

TEST: Unit 4, Pages 27–28, Teacher's Guide

1. A	**10.** A	**19.** A
2. D	**11.** B	**20.** B
3. C	**12.** C	**21.** C
4. C	**13.** C	**22.** C
5. C	**14.** A	**23.** D
6. B	**15.** D	**24.** A
7. A	**16.** A	**25.** D
8. D	**17.** A	**26.** B
9. B	**18.** D	

TEST: Unit 5, Pages 29–30, Teacher's Guide

1. A	**9.** A	**17.** D
2. D	**10.** B	**18.** D
3. C	**11.** C	**19.** C
4. A	**12.** A	**20.** A
5. D	**13.** B	
6. D	**14.** B	
7. C	**15.** A	
8. A	**16.** D	

TEST: Unit 6, Pages 31–32, Teacher's Guide

1. D	**9.** C	**17.** D
2. A	**10.** A	**18.** C
3. B	**11.** B	**19.** A
4. C	**12.** C	**20.** D
5. A	**13.** D	**21.** C
6. D	**14.** A	**22.** B
7. B	**15.** A	
8. A	**16.** B	

Choose the correct answer to each question.

Which word pairs are synonyms?

1. A ○ remain, see
   B ○ remain, stay
   C ○ remain, visit
   D ○ remain, avoid

2. A ○ throw, ball
   B ○ throw, pitch
   C ○ throw, run
   D ○ throw, threw

3. A ○ nation, country
   B ○ nation, world
   C ○ nation, city
   D ○ nation, state

4. A ○ simple, stupid
   B ○ simple, hard
   C ○ simple, wrong
   D ○ simple, easy

Which word pairs are antonyms?

5. A ○ cry, laugh
   B ○ cry, sing
   C ○ cry, hear
   D ○ cry, cough

6. A ○ smile, sing
   B ○ smile, lick
   C ○ smile, frown
   D ○ smile, weep

7. A ○ buy, by
   B ○ buy, sell
   C ○ buy, busy
   D ○ buy, greet

8. A ○ under, below
   B ○ under, stand
   C ○ under, cover
   D ○ under, over

Choose the homonym for each underlined word.

9. <u>hear</u>
   A ○ ear　C ○ here
   B ○ there　D ○ next

10. <u>too</u>
   A ○ also　C ○ one
   B ○ two　D ○ from

11. <u>its</u>
   A ○ his　C ○ hers
   B ○ it's　D ○ ours

12. <u>their</u>
   A ○ they're　C ○ our
   B ○ here　D ○ were

13. <u>write</u>
   A ○ wrong　C ○ left
   B ○ record　D ○ right

14. <u>there</u>
   A ○ here　C ○ their
   B ○ now　D ○ then

Name ______________________________

Choose the correct meaning for each underlined word.

15. He filled the hole with dirt.
   - A ○ entire thing
   - B ○ box
   - C ○ empty space
   - D ○ wagon

16. She wore a plain dress.
   - A ○ striped
   - B ○ white
   - C ○ flat surface
   - D ○ not fancy

17. The plants were in rows.
   - A ○ straight lines
   - B ○ moves with oars
   - C ○ flowers
   - D ○ roads

18. We beat the other team.
   - A ○ a red vegetable
   - B ○ hit
   - C ○ won against
   - D ○ lost

Choose the correct meaning for each underlined word.

19. refill
   - A ○ not full
   - B ○ fill
   - C ○ empty
   - D ○ fill again

20. careful
   - A ○ reckless
   - B ○ full of care
   - C ○ care again
   - D ○ without care

21. unhappy
   - A ○ with joy
   - B ○ glad
   - C ○ not happy
   - D ○ happy again

22. careless
   - A ○ cautious
   - B ○ without care
   - C ○ safe
   - D ○ mean

23. misspell
   - A ○ spell wrong
   - B ○ write
   - C ○ spell again
   - D ○ careless

24. disagree
   - A ○ cross
   - B ○ complain
   - C ○ angry
   - D ○ not agree

Choose the two words that can be combined to make a compound word.

25.
   - A ○ under, over
   - B ○ black, sea
   - C ○ open, door
   - D ○ air, plane

26.
   - A ○ quick, fast
   - B ○ shoe, lace
   - C ○ did, not
   - D ○ some, many

27.
   - A ○ door, knob
   - B ○ shoe, sock
   - C ○ hat, coat
   - D ○ them, they

Choose the two words that can be combined to make the underlined contraction.

28. Murray said he'd need more time.
   - A ○ he will
   - B ○ he would
   - C ○ he could
   - D ○ he did

29. He isn't finished with his project.
   - A ○ are not
   - B ○ is not
   - C ○ he is
   - D ○ I will

30. They'd go if they could.
   - A ○ They have
   - B ○ They would
   - C ○ They did
   - D ○ We would

31. You'd better be nice!
   - A ○ You will
   - B ○ You were
   - C ○ You are
   - D ○ You had

32. We'll wait until tomorrow.
   - A ○ We would
   - B ○ We were
   - C ○ We are
   - D ○ We will

33. It shouldn't be much longer.
   - A ○ should let
   - B ○ should have
   - C ○ should not
   - D ○ shall not

 Name ____________________

Choose the group of words that is a sentence.

1. A ○ Wanted more time.
   B ○ Said our story.
   C ○ That he couldn't wait.
   D ○ He saved for a new car.

2. A ○ She almost.
   B ○ Diane worked hard.
   C ○ Late every day.
   D ○ She was very.

3. A ○ The horse grazed.
   B ○ On green grass.
   C ○ Ate a great deal.
   D ○ Ran around.

4. A ○ Asked a question.
   B ○ The answer.
   C ○ Told the truth.
   D ○ You were right.

Choose whether each sentence is declarative, interrogative, imperative, or exclamatory.

5. Did you study for the test?
   A ○ declarative
   B ○ interrogative
   C ○ imperative
   D ○ exclamatory

6. Oh, no, I forgot the test!
   A ○ declarative
   B ○ interrogative
   C ○ imperative
   D ○ exclamatory

7. Answer these questions.
   A ○ declarative
   B ○ interrogative
   C ○ imperative
   D ○ exclamatory

8. I don't know if I can.
   A ○ declarative
   B ○ interrogative
   C ○ imperative
   D ○ exclamatory

Choose the sentence that changes the underlined sentence to the type of sentence in parentheses.

9. Hand me that bowl. (interrogative)
   A ○ Give me that bowl.
   B ○ Hand me that bowl!
   C ○ Will you hand me that bowl?
   D ○ You handed me that bowl.

10. Did you pick up the mail? (declarative)
    A ○ You picked up the mail.
    B ○ Pick up the mail.
    C ○ Will you pick up the mail?
    D ○ Hurry and pick up the mail!

11. Would you like to go to a movie? (imperative)
    A ○ You would like to go to a movie.
    B ○ Are you going to a movie?
    C ○ Go to a movie.
    D ○ Let's go to a movie!

12. I think I'm lost. (exclamatory)
    A ○ Am I lost?
    B ○ I am lost.
    C ○ Don't tell me I'm lost.
    D ○ I'm lost!

Name ______________________________

Choose the correct answer to each question.

13. Which sentence has the subject underlined?
   - A ○ Jerry needed a research project.
   - B ○ He didn't have an idea.
   - C ○ He thought about electricity.
   - D ○ Cindi gave him some ideas.

14. Which sentence has the simple subject underlined?
   - A ○ He couldn't decide.
   - B ○ He needed more time.
   - C ○ Jerry went to Cindi.
   - D ○ She said she would help.

15. Which sentence has the simple subject and the simple predicate underlined?
   - A ○ The cat jumped on the bed.
   - B ○ It was running from the dog.
   - C ○ The dog chased it.
   - D ○ The cat was finally safe.

16. Which sentence has the simple predicate underlined?
   - A ○ Cindi asked him what he liked.
   - B ○ She asked him questions.
   - C ○ They chose three subjects.
   - D ○ Jerry had to pick one of them.

17. Which sentence has the predicate underlined?
   - A ○ He still couldn't decide.
   - B ○ Jerry went to the library.
   - C ○ He saw many books on engines.
   - D ○ Jerry finally picked engines.

18. Which sentence has the subject and the predicate underlined?
   - A ○ Mary found a wooden chest.
   - B ○ Her sister helped her open it.
   - C ○ They found an old diary in there.
   - D ○ They read it with interest.

Choose the sentence that is a simple sentence.

19. A ○ We can run, or we can walk.
   - B ○ Let's walk together.
   - C ○ You are fast, and I am slow.
   - D ○ He will run, so I'll follow.

Choose the sentence that is a compound sentence.

20. A ○ I'll do it that way.
   - B ○ You can watch me.
   - C ○ I'll start it, and you can finish it.
   - D ○ It's not the same.

Choose the sentence that correctly combines each set of sentences.

21. We bought a house. It is white. It is big.
   - A ○ The big white house is ours.
   - B ○ We bought a big white house.
   - C ○ We bought a new house.
   - D ○ Is our house big and white?

22. She sold her book. It is a novel. It is new.
   - A ○ Her novel is new.
   - B ○ Her new book is a novel.
   - C ○ She sold her new novel.
   - D ○ Did she sell her new novel?

 Name ____________________

Choose the correct plural form of each underlined singular noun.

1. country
   A ○ countreys B ○ countrys C ○ countries D ○ country's

2. box
   A ○ boxys B ○ boxs C ○ boxies D ○ boxes

3. calf
   A ○ calfs B ○ calvs C ○ calves D ○ calfies

4. woman
   A ○ women B ○ womyn C ○ wimmin D ○ woman's

Choose the phrase that shows the correct possessive for each underlined phrase.

5. the hat of my father
   A ○ the hat's of my father
   B ○ my fathers' hat
   C ○ my father's hats
   D ○ my father's hat

6. the pages of the book
   A ○ the book's pages'
   B ○ the books' pages
   C ○ the book page's
   D ○ the book's pages

Choose the sentence that has an action verb.

7. A ○ Rain is water.
   B ○ Rain falls from the sky.
   C ○ Rain feels soft on my face.
   D ○ Rain had been expected.

8. A ○ Lee kicked the ball.
   B ○ Lee is tired.
   C ○ Lee has been working hard.
   D ○ Lee became sleepy.

Choose the sentence that has a linking verb.

9. A ○ We had been waiting.
   B ○ We grew impatient.
   C ○ We called the number.
   D ○ We asked for George.

10. A ○ Erin is talented.
    B ○ Erin wants to be a star.
    C ○ Erin sings and dances.
    D ○ Erin even tells jokes.

Choose the sentence that has a helping verb.

11. A ○ Dirk has gone for help.
    B ○ Dirk seemed sad.
    C ○ Dirk pulled his jacket on.
    D ○ Dirk walked away.

12. A ○ I accepted an invitation.
    B ○ It sounded like fun.
    C ○ I looked at my calendar.
    D ○ I am going tomorrow.

Name ______________________________

Choose the correct verb to complete each sentence.

13. Regina and Tony _____ cousins.
   - A ○ are
   - B ○ is
   - C ○ was
   - D ○ am

14. Todd and I _____ each other.
   - A ○ seen
   - B ○ has seen
   - C ○ saw
   - D ○ have saw

15. You already _____ me some.
   - A ○ have gave
   - B ○ gave
   - C ○ given
   - D ○ give

16. They _____ each other every summer.
   - A ○ sees
   - B ○ visits
   - C ○ visiting
   - D ○ visit

17. When will you _____ her again?
   - A ○ had seen
   - B ○ seen
   - C ○ see
   - D ○ saw

18. I _____ to visit you.
   - A ○ have came
   - B ○ came
   - C ○ had coming
   - D ○ coming

Choose the correct pronoun to complete each sentence.

19. _____ runs in many races.
   - A ○ We
   - B ○ Him
   - C ○ He
   - D ○ I

20. All of _____ grapes were ripe.
   - A ○ mine
   - B ○ him
   - C ○ them
   - D ○ my

21. We told _____.
   - A ○ they
   - B ○ them
   - C ○ he
   - D ○ she

22. _____ heel was broken.
   - A ○ Her
   - B ○ She
   - C ○ Them
   - D ○ Our

23. That looks like _____ son.
   - A ○ its
   - B ○ them
   - C ○ their
   - D they

Choose the correct adjective or adverb to complete each sentence.

24. The giraffe is the _____ animal.
   - A ○ tall
   - B ○ taller
   - C ○ tallest
   - D ○ tallness

25. The blue whale is _____ than any other mammal.
   - A ○ biggest
   - B ○ big
   - C ○ bigly
   - D ○ bigger

26. She plays the piano very _____.
   - A ○ good
   - B ○ better
   - C ○ well
   - D ○ best

27. Don't you have _____ family?
   - A ○ any
   - B ○ no
   - C ○ none
   - D ○ no one

28. The phone rang _____.
   - A ○ sudden
   - B ○ loud
   - C ○ suddenly
   - D ○ jarring

Name ______________________________

Choose the correct answer to each question.

In which sentence are the words capitalized correctly?

1. A ○ Rebecca likes people.
   B ○ She has many Friends.
   C ○ Her friends Like her.
   D ○ Rebecca is a Computer Operator.

2. A ○ The empire state building is tall.
   B ○ It Looms over New York city.
   C ○ you can go up to the top.
   D ○ Can you see the Atlantic Ocean?

3. A ○ The Lawyer made a joke.
   B ○ Judge hardy laughed.
   C ○ The judge's dog, Ripper, growled.
   D ○ Judge Hardy told ripper to be quiet.

Which sentence is written correctly?

4. A ○ "Mary will you show us the pictures
   B ○ Sure, said Mary I'll be glad to.
   C ○ "These are great," Alice said.
   D ○ "It was a lot of fun" said Mary

5. A ○ "Let me go, said Eileen.
   B ○ Chuck said, "I'll come, too.
   C ○ "I want to be alone," she said.
   D ○ Okay, said Chuck.

Which sentence needs a comma?

6. A ○ Sue came home on Friday.
   B ○ She was tired but she was happy.
   C ○ Everyone was glad to see her.
   D ○ They planned a party for her.

7. A ○ He was tired so he took a nap.
   B ○ He slept all afternoon.
   C ○ He snored and dreamed.
   D ○ He remembered his dream.

Which greeting is written correctly?

8. A ○ dear Tina,
   B ○ Dear Tina
   C ○ Dear Ms. Jones
   D ○ Dear Ms. Jones,

9. A ○ dear marsha,
   B ○ Dear Marsha,
   C ○ Dear marsha
   D ○ Dear Marsha

Which closing is written correctly?

10. A ○ Sincerely yours,
    B ○ Sincerely Yours,
    C ○ Sincerely yours
    D ○ sincerely yours,

11. A ○ yours truly,
    B ○ Yours truly,
    C ○ Yours truly
    D ○ your's Truly,

12. Which address is written correctly?
    A ○ 4700 w greenwood
    Park Ridge, il 60030
    B ○ 1023 North lamar
    austin, TX 78767
    C ○ 7280 N. Martin
    Boulder, CO 72815
    D ○ 871 W. Oak
    Boston Ma 01340

Name ______________________________

Choose the sentence that is punctuated correctly.

13. A ○ Will help.
    B ○ Would you like to sit here.
    C ○ Where are you going?
    D ○ How are you!

14. A ○ Don't cut yourself!
    B ○ Is it sharp.
    C ○ Very sharp.
    D ○ I'll be careful?

Choose the two words that make each underlined contraction.

15. <u>we're</u>

A ○ we will	C ○ we would
B ○ we have	D ○ we are

16. <u>it's</u>

A ○ it is	C ○ it did
B ○ it was	D ○ it will

Choose the phrase in which the apostrophe is used correctly.

17. A ○ didn't know how
    B ○ the meetings members
    C ○ lets' go
    D ○ it's leg

18. A ○ Helens' daughter
    B ○ was'nt there
    C ○ lost shoe's
    D ○ farmer's cattle

19. A ○ do'nt worry
    B ○ his money's worth
    C ○ shouldnt' care
    D ○ Lizs' address

Choose the sentence that needs a capital letter.

20. A ○ Sara was on vacation.
    B ○ She went to mt. Rushmore.
    C ○ She studied its history.
    D ○ Mt. Rushmore is very famous.

21. A ○ Abraham Lincoln is one of the faces.
    B ○ Abe is famous, too.
    C ○ He was president of the united states.
    D ○ President Lincoln was a kind man.

Choose the two words that make each underlined contraction.

22. <u>I'm</u>

A ○ I will	C ○ I am
B ○ I would	D ○ I have

23. <u>won't</u>

A ○ would not	C ○ do not
B ○ did not	D ○ will not

Choose the phrase in which the apostrophe is used correctly.

24. A ○ couldn't find it
    B ○ that beaches' sand
    C ○ times' flying
    D ○ going to Wesleys'

25. A ○ flie's wings
    B ○ up in arms'
    C ○ Marias' car
    D ○ boxes' lids

26. A ○ countrie's flag
    B ○ they'll stay
    C ○ is'nt gone
    D ○ up the stair's

 Name ________________________

Read the paragraphs. Then answer the questions.

A

Vince had a plan. First, he would get a job. Then he would save all his money. Next, he would buy a car. Vince's brother has a car.

1. What is the topic sentence in paragraph A?
   A ○ Vince had a plan.
   B ○ First, he would get a job.
   C ○ Then he would save all his money.
   D ○ Next, he would buy a car.

2. Which sentence in paragraph A does not give supporting details?
   A ○ Then, he would save all his money.
   B ○ First, he would get a job.
   C ○ Next, he would buy a car.
   D ○ Vince's brother has a car.

3. Which form of punctuation is used around a quote, in all paragraphs?
   A ○ periods
   B ○ commas
   C ○ quotation marks
   D ○ question marks

B

The plan had some problems. Vince didn't make enough money. Cars are all very expensive. He bought a gift with his money. Vince's birthday was last week.

4. What is the topic sentence in paragraph B?
   A ○ The plan had some problems.
   B ○ Vince didn't make enough money.
   C ○ Cars are all very expensive.
   D ○ He bought a gift with his money.

5. Which sentence in paragraph B does not give supporting details?
   A ○ Vince didn't make enough money.
   B ○ Cars are all very expensive.
   C ○ He bought a gift with his money.
   D ○ Vince's birthday was last week.

6. What should you consider when writing a paragraph?
   A ○ only your interests
   B ○ when it will be read
   C ○ books you've read lately
   D ○ the audience

Choose the time order word from each sentence.

7. Then he saved money.
   A ○ he **C** ○ Then
   B ○ money **D** ○ saved

8. Finally, he got to buy a car.
   A ○ Finally **C** ○ car
   B ○ buy **D** ○ got

9. Afterward, he said goodbye.
   A ○ Afterward **C** ○ said
   B ○ he **D** ○ goodbye

10. Next, he will save for clothes.
    A ○ save **C** ○ clothes
    B ○ Next **D** ○ for

Name ______________________________

Read the conversation. Then answer the questions.

I don't know what to do, said José.
"What's the problem" asked Lonny.
José said, "I can't decide whether to go to the movie or to the race. They both sound like fun."
"Why don't you go to the movie tomorrow? Surely it will be playing then."
"That is a great idea!"

11. What punctuation is missing from the first sentence?

A ○ question mark
B ○ exclamation point
C ○ quotation marks
D ○ comma

12. Who says the movie and the race sound like fun?

A ○ José **C** ○ I
B ○ Lonny **D** ○ They

13. What is the simple subject of the first sentence?

A ○ José **C** ○ what
B ○ I **D** ○ do

14. What punctuation should come after the word "problem"?

A ○ comma
B ○ question mark
C ○ period
D ○ exclamation point

15. Who says going to the movie tomorrow is a great idea?

A ○ José **C** ○ I
B ○ Lonny **D** ○ They

16. What is the simple predicate of the last sentence?

A ○ idea **C** ○ great
B ○ that **D** ○ is

Study the following outline. Then answer the questions.

Statement: Saving natural resources

I. Problems
  A. Pollution
    1. air
    2.
    3. land
  B.
    1. food
    2. paper
    3.
    4. plastics
II. Solutions
  A. Conservation
  B.

17. What best fits as subheading I. A. 2.?

A ○ wastes **C** ○ garbage
B ○ oil **D** ○ water

18. What best fits as subheading I. B.?

A ○ Oceans **C** ○ Deserts
B ○ Rain Forests **D** ○ Wastes

19. What best fits as subheading I. B. 3.?

A ○ plants **C** ○ glass
B ○ doors **D** ○ toys

20. What best fits as subheading II. B.?

A ○ Recycling **C** ○ Burying
B ○ Piling **D** ○ Burning

 Name ______________________

Choose the correct answer to each question.

1. Which word would be on a page with the guide words **able / again**?

   A ○ a C ○ alone
   B ○ ago D ○ afford

2. Which word would be on a page with the guide words **cold / contest**?

   A ○ come C ○ code
   B ○ coin D ○ corn

3. Which group of words is in correct alphabetical order?

   A ○ cub, cure, cry, cup
   B ○ debt, deck, deep, den
   C ○ girl, glad, giggle, glue
   D ○ is, iron, it, isn't

4. Which group of words is in correct alphabetical order?

   A ○ behold, believe, begin, bee
   B ○ chose, chat, cave, chef
   C ○ dot, doze, every, fog
   D ○ apple, bear, big, bang

5. Which respelling is correct for the word slam?

   A ○ slăm C ○ sləm
   B ○ slām D ○ slum

6. What does the abbreviation adj. stand for?

   A ○ verb C ○ noun
   B ○ adverb D ○ adjective

Use the sample encyclopedia article to answer the questions.

> **COAL** is a natural, black carbon solid used as fuel. For years it was our prime source of power. It is found underground and is made from layers of dead plants. *See also* FUEL.

7. What is the article about?

   A ○ fuel C ○ dead plants
   B ○ coal D ○ carbon

8. What is the cross-reference?

   A ○ fuel C ○ underground
   B ○ carbon D ○ layers

9. Where is coal found?

   A ○ fuel C ○ underground
   B ○ carbon D ○ layers

10. What is coal made from?

    A ○ dead plants C ○ power
    B ○ fuel D ○ underground

Name ______________________________

Choose the correct definition for the underlined word in each sentence.

11. The punch made perfect holes in the paper.
    - A ○ a beverage with fruit juice
    - B ○ a tool for making holes
    - C ○ energy
    - D ○ a blow with the fist

12. The four-year-old is full of punch.
    - A ○ a beverage with fruit juice
    - B ○ a tool for making holes
    - C ○ energy
    - D ○ a blow with the fist

13. The strong punch to his head made him fall down.
    - A ○ a beverage with fruit juice
    - B ○ a tool for making holes
    - C ○ energy
    - D ○ a blow with the fist

14. She served cranberry punch.
    - A ○ a beverage with fruit juice
    - B ○ a tool for making holes
    - C ○ energy
    - D ○ a blow with the fist

Choose the correct answer to each question about encyclopedias.

15. To find an article on the life of NASA astronaut John Glenn, which word would you look under?
    - A ○ Glenn
    - B ○ astronaut
    - C ○ John
    - D ○ NASA

16. To find an article about the different uses for diamonds, which word would you look under?
    - A ○ gems
    - B ○ diamonds
    - C ○ mining
    - D ○ uses

17. Which volume would have an article about the mythical character Paul Bunyan?
    - A ○ M
    - B ○ P
    - C ○ C
    - D ○ B

18. Which volume would have an article about the flight of whooping cranes in America?
    - A ○ C
    - B ○ A
    - C ○ W
    - D ○ F

Choose the page in a book where each group of underlined words would be found.

19. The author's name
    - A ○ title page
    - B ○ index
    - C ○ copyright page
    - D ○ table of contents

20. A chapter title
    - A ○ title page
    - B ○ index
    - C ○ copyright page
    - D ○ table of contents

21. The year the book was published
    - A ○ title page
    - B ○ index
    - C ○ copyright page
    - D ○ table of contents

22. Page number for certain information
    - A ○ title page
    - B ○ index
    - C ○ copyright page
    - D ○ table of contents

 Name ______________________